BAD ANIMAL

Kathryn Bratt-Pfotenhauer

Riot in Your Throat
publishing fierce, feminist poetry

Bratt-Pfotenhauer, Kathryn.
1st edition.
ISBN: 978-1-7361386-8-7

Cover Art: Oscar Keys (www.unsplash.com)
Cover Design: Kirsten Birst
Book Design: Shanna Compton
Author Photo: Tracy Xue

Riot in Your Throat
Arlington, VA
www.riotinyourthroat.com

For Mikaela—

CONTENTS

PRAYER

Like this, the dead elk was deposited onto the tarp:
rain crowned its antlers, the scruff under

its neck glistened with dew. In murder, as in living,
the animal sound was paramount, the death-cry, the orgasm,

how we communicated we were in danger, or pleasure. I heard
nature cry out that day. What it meant, I still don't know. The birds

lifted from the trees, an eyelid fluttering open.
The trees shuddered their leaves against the blood spatter.

I was younger then. I knew nothing of death except my father
wielding the rifle, then the knife. My hand gently patted

the elk's dead, dead flank as my father grabbed a handful
of its hair and held it steady, began to cut. I thought I was

comforting it, or maybe I was comforting myself.
Nothing will be wasted this way, I thought. *Nothing left.*

Silence in the car as we drove home, the elk in the backseat,
blood pooling in its two tusked ivory teeth. I have the luxury

of writing about this violence in hypotheticals. We never
killed the elk. We never opened the animal from sternum

to groin to see what organs lay beneath; we were never
that fascinated with our own bodies, their sounds. The elk was dead

when we got there. The blood already seeped into the soil.
Tiny animals already made their homes in the bones. Eyes

had become less than eyes. A cluster of maggots peered through the flesh
shyly, like girls around a velvet curtain at a ballet recital.

We didn't know what to do with ourselves, or the body, so we left it
there. I could say something about nature taking itself back. I could

say something about the murder. Here it is:
nothing was wasted, nothing was left. But—

in the center of its forehead,
a bullet nestled like a small child.

SELF-PORTRAIT AS MOIROLOGIST

It's my job to mourn. To wear black
like my father wore black, to stalk and bawl
behind a hearse as it makes its slow crawl
towards the cemetery. And when I watched
the crows gather, they watched me too.
We stood there, observing each other as around us,
a clique of corpses was laid to rest. And when one bird
fell from the line in a burst of electricity and feathers, I ran
to catch it. Paid the rest of the murder no mind
as they surrounded their dead friend and cawed,
pecked my hands when I got too close. Everyone
mourns differently. Some are the carrion birds and some
are carrion, the difference barely palpable. I cannot shake
the feeling I will die soon. In the incredible inky
darkness of night, I am holding a man to my chest, hoping
he doesn't wake to a body. I am holding a bird in my hands
and watching it die.

THE UNDISCOVERED COUNTRY

I break the skull of the dead bird with my foot. The moon
a pale eye of fat in a sky buoyed by stars. Fields, slicked dark

with rain. How often have I come like a pilgrim
to this place? There is wind here, life here. A breeze picks

my hair like a comb. Iris, crocus, growing through animal bones.
The world goes on around us, even when we depart it.

The river empties its hands over and over again.
The orchard drops fruit like a hemline over the grass,

each apple pitted with rot, each pomegranate broken open
to reveal a pair of lips. There is something to be said about the heaven

we imagine, and the heaven we get. How
we interpret the profound silence of God.

I have lived in this silence so I might answer to it,
come to this place so I may answer you when you ask.

This is the country they call death.
See me walk towards it.

THE EXECUTIONER'S WIFE

In his black suit, in his black coat, he could be
anything. A man with a gaunt face. A man alone,

twiddling fingers, sharpening the blade. Who
among us has done no harm? A man sharpens a blade,

and it is alive and scything in his hand. A man guts
an animal and calls it a man, calls it deserved. We are not here

to judge. Unpleasantness, or murder is an unfortunate fact
of life. I wonder what my life would have been like without

his hair in the shower drain, the fingerprints on the wall
as he brought me to bed. His bloody gloves discarded

on the floor as I kissed him and kissed him again. Every
morning, his hands in my hair, his fingers on my neck: its black electricity.

His cry of pleasure was every voice lifted to God's ear. Yes,
we still believe in a God that forgives. Doesn't everyone?

IN THE MORGUE

I was a student. I knew death, knew it as one knows the slip
of skin against skin, something bloodclose, natural. I knew

the false rot of formaldehyde, could see the mortician's tools
in their little silver dish: aneurysm hook, drain tube, trocar.

The man on the table could have been my brother, or my father,
I loved him that much, the feeling arterial. I knew him

and yet did not know him. I pulled open the eyelids,
stuck in the eye caps, with their tiny

and uniform spikes. I called myself patient. I called myself
saved. I hoped at the end of life, there was more life, but

I didn't have my hopes up.
I did my job. But—

I held his hand. I held
his hand in my hand.

DESAIROLOGY

It's a question of appearances. In London, there's a clown egg
registry. Each egg painted with a clown's likeness, each put under glass.
Something about protecting copyright. Each day, I put on my makeup,
paint my face as if for a funeral. This is how I want to be
remembered, lips colored peach or plum or gunmetal blue.
I won't have control over how or when I go, but this, I can do
right. I can primp and pluck, polish my nails, my teeth. This
is how I will face death: with my face on. My father told me
when I was eight about what he wanted when he died. Me, tiny crypt keeper.
Groucho Marx glasses and the theme from Local Hero. He wanted
everyone to be laughing, joking. And now, he is 77 and death
creeps over his apartment like a blush. His friend Barbara
didn't come home from the hospital and he is still calling.
Each morning, the dial tone. Each morning, laughter in the other room.

READING *FRANKENSTEIN* IN SEPTEMBER

Let me say that I too wanted to die. Wanted
to abandon my post, listening at the bathroom door

for the sound of my father finishing his work, expelling
the body's refuse. I listened not out of a curiosity, but out

of warning: an assurance he wouldn't fall, or hit his head
on something. I listened to ensure one of us lived.

There was no snow-slicked tundra here, no ship locked
in the embrace of ice. In fact, I sweated through my shirt,

the last, hot tongues of summer teasing along my neck.
My father kept the apartment chilled, a bottle of white wine

held at the closure. And when I cut his toenails, I did so
with the devotion of a child confronted with their father's mortality

for the first time: fearful, a little nervous. I shouldn't
have worried. The clippers sliced through the thickened edge

of the nail efficiently. Their sick noise sounded in the silence,
while I knelt at the foot of my creator. I could have spent my life stitching

what is precious together again: the line between my first initial
and the middle name of his other daughter, the one who died.

I could have spent my life chasing the ideal female:
her name was Rebecca. Her little fists opened and closed,

then opened again. Her lungs: little birds in flight.

PASTORAL WITH BIRDS

I crept into the November night to watch. The door opened, bent
like a broken finger, and outside, the first snow of the season,
blanching the concrete. My old car in the lot, dusted, as though with
confectioner's sugar and rusted from nineteen years of travel. My feet, traveled
and bone-sore, toes curled against the cold. And around me in that darkness,
the chittering of small creatures: a black squirrel scavenging the ground,
in the trees, miscellaneous birds. I have measured the years
by the beating of their wings, by the worms bisected in their
beaks. I watched them scrabble in the winter months: the waxwing,
the cardinal, the American robin. Once, a snowy owl perched
on the branch of a dead tree in my front yard, and I thought its tracks were
the handwriting of God. This had something to do with my dying grandmother
and symbolism I think, the picture my father had sent me, where she was hooked
to the world by a needle in her arm: red tube against white sheets, like the
chokeberry bush outside my childhood home against snow. I waited
for the season to deliver me to a better understanding. I fed the owl: a mouse had died
behind the kitchen cabinets. For days I wondered where the death-smell
was coming from, and when I found it, I wondered how I hadn't heard it
squeaking, and how it died alone, not unlike my grandmother. I carried it out
with a pair of tongs. I left it on the garden path. I let nature do its yearning,
bloody work, watched the owl devour the body of the mouse and felt nothing
except a singular kind of regret: that I was not small enough to warrant
such a dispatch, that I had not died too, and what's more, my death would not
be useful. It would be just a death. The bird, just a bird.

DRIVING TO MEADVILLE

20 miles outside Buffalo, I smell
smoke. A truck is stalled, dismembered
by the curve of the road's shoulder, the parts
strewn about like freckles on a lover. The back half
is a constellation of flame. The driver, despondent,
is on his phone, calling, I imagine, a superior,
or calling, I imagine, the police, the fire engines
that almost certainly won't get there in time to save his cargo.
And when I arrive in Meadville, where my sister
studies stars and gamma rays and all things physical,
I will tell her about the truck, the man, how close
I came to burning. She will look at me with concern, and shudder.
And weeks from then, after Christmas and New Year's have come
and gone, there will be wildfires so close to my old neighbors' home
they can be seen from the front porch blackening the hillside, and the wife
will tell us a cell from her uterus has become a comet,
migrating to her liver, her lung, and begun the awful work
of metastasizing. And my mother just buried a friend
from college who died of a cancer in a matter
of weeks, and I am helpless in the face of all this grief,
its face so like the driver when he realized
he had lost everything.

BURIAL

When Winston died, we planted a garden, kept
his sweaters in a box. His collar we put on a stuffed lookalike

my sister sleeps with when she's home. When he died,
the vet came personally to the house. When he died,

my sister would not let anyone see her grief. She bore
his body upstairs, wouldn't come down for hours. You have

to understand: he was terminal two different ways.
There was no story that ended happily for him, no miracle.

My father, who never wanted a dog after a series of childhood pets
ended up under tires, cried with the rest of us as he stopped panting,

repeated how he was sorry, so sorry. Grief was the dog
running. Grief was the slip of the needle beneath skin. So

we planted a garden. We buy flowers for the dog every summer, forget-
me-nots. Today, my grandfather calls me because there's a need

for genetic testing. His cancer is back, and with it
inheritance matters: who gets what piece of this particularly

unfortunate pie. Apparently, my mother is refusing to test, or not
testing as soon as they'd like. And who doesn't want their children

to outlive them? Their grandchildren? My grandparents already
have their burial plots picked out. One family reunion, we stooped

in the Illinois dirt to take pictures where our smiles beamed wide over
our teeth next to their graves, the place where I will one day go

to show my children I was loved once, and that I loved.

THE CONTRACT

after Sylvia Plath

God, were I more like You
I might care less about the world.
Might care more instead about the safe
chalk mess of children
on the sidewalk

coloring their small, incredible lives
green and pink and running home
with hands dusted in glitter.
I address the hypothetical infants:
My children, my children—

how I wish the world for them.
I wish them candles, a light
that doesn't falter in the deadpan
drum of the future, death darkening
into a faded spot on an old shirt.

Any creator worth their salt
has an obligation to uphold,
has opted into an agreement.
It is why I am terrified of
my children, my children—

I owe them a future, like how You
up there owe me the benefit
of Your creation. I do not ask much.
I do not ask much at all. I only ask that
You honor the contract.

THE ART PARK

The seas are rising, and the world is half-dead, and Jill and I have driven forty minutes outside the city to look at sculptures. There is a twisted floral thing painted silver; it sways with each gust, the wind breathing at our shins like a huffy toddler. The clouds pile up in cigarette rolls. Off to the side, there is a wire door with wire steps that opens into nothing, and Jill makes a joke about Narnia, about alternate realities. There is a sign that says not to touch or sit on the artwork. I have a mind to do it, just do it, there's no one around to see me except for the compostable toilet and Jill, but I won't. There are some things that are still sacred, there is still something worth saving, and sometimes that has to be enough. Jill's hand points at a wire horse rearing in the middle of the field. It looks like it could buck you, it looks like it could bite. It looks like it could do a lot of things. My hand hangs empty in the air, so lonely I could almost cry. I look at videos from New York where the subways are submerged and in Philly, people are cannonballing into the sewage water in swim trunks. It is hard not to feel slightly anxious about this. I am clutching a stress ball the size of my fist, meaning I am clutching my fist. I am debating whether it's even ethical to have children anymore, is it responsible. I am writing letters to my imaginary son. I call him Felix. It means lucky.

PRAYER

Approaching twenty-five, and still with a hope
of children, I sit in the doctor's office.

Around me, the world bubbles in its clay pot. Late
summer, and the heat—

enough to kill someone. I read statistics on my phone,
scrolling through stories of kids strapped in hot cars, unable

to get out. Each passing summer, it gets hotter. I name
the bloody rags of my underwear as the deluge comes:

Miranda. James. Elise. Red ribbons down my legs. It shouldn't
mean anything anymore. At least, not like it once did. Confession:

I got on my knees the other day for a man. I let him do
things to me and feigned desire but didn't want it.

I spent the days after clutching a test and praying
that I stayed empty. It was negative. To believe in anything

at all requires suspension. To believe in something higher
than your own capacity for creation would stump anyone.

The older woman next to me saw me cradling
my stomach. I imagine I looked scared. She put a hand

on mine. Told me I'd be just fine. God: she wore
a paisley shirt and blue jeans. She looked like my mother,

or maybe just any mother.

THE HYRTL SKULL COLLECTION

We are admiring the skull collection
when an ice pick drills itself into

my temple. I am sick of headaches,
and the headaches are sick of me, my unfortunate

genetics wedding me to pain like they did
my mother, my grandmother: inheritance and curse.

Staring at me, 139 skulls collected to disprove
phrenology, which dictated that

cranial features determined intellect. Read: racist,
bunk, awful. *A philosophy,* Hyrtl said, *that*

could only be invented by idiots for idiots.
My skull and I, we are staring

at human remains; people. They were once
people. They have names, are labeled; black ink

decorates their foreheads in the manner of the specimen.
It is a known collection. We know things about these people.

Andrew Sokoloff died castrating himself.
Marianna Corti died of childbed fever.

She and I are the same age. I am
wondering if her child made it, who they became

if they became anything at all. I want children.
I want. My mother asks if I want

them for the right reasons, and I don't know
what they are. I don't know

what to tell her. I want, but am reluctant
to pass on this pain, this cranial ricochet.

Everybody deals with pain, my mother says.
You just get better at hiding it.

THE SPIDER

I saw it before he did. The spider, on the move,
dropping from the rim of the toilet, small
and assured. Harmless, he assured me. The belt
of its web strung from its spinnerets. My hand
itching for the toggle to send it spinning down
the drain, so I wouldn't have to see it drown.

And suddenly, the memory of almost drowning
in the river, when I was young and stupid. We moved
as one in those days, a pack of teenagers playing at going down
to the rocky shore of the water, playing chicken, small
on the bank. When the park ranger found us, his hand
came down hard on someone's arm, his belt

glittering in the afternoon light, a sunbelt
all its own. We pled our youth. We'd rather have drowned
than faced our parents and their anger and their hands,
the quickness of the punishment waiting for us as we moved
towards the mouth of the park again, sullen, soggy, and small.
I lied to my mother. She looked me in the face, looked down

at my clothes and told me I better not have been down
to the river, better not have gone swimming. The belt
of her lips opened to issue a warning: *I will make you small.*
I will make you listen. Do you know how many people drown
in that river every year? My mother, who moved
to block my path, eyes hard like little river rocks, her hands

gripping my shoulders. I've never known desperation like that, hands
like bear traps. Then again, I've never had a child. Never gone down
to the hospital and walked out with a heart outside my chest, moving
and breathing and beating tiny fists against me, belted
into a car seat or tucked into a crib. I didn't drown
in the river. But I never left the water, stayed there soft and small.

When I was a child, I tried very hard to die. Took my small
cousin to the point in the lake where water became black. His hands
beat on my breast trying to get back. He didn't want to drown.
And he didn't. That's not how this story ends. I stopped sinking down
and trudged to shore. My uncle, shaking his head, loosening his belt,
his hand tensing against my cheek. My body, devoid of movement.

I stayed small in the water, went down. Didn't speak
for the hand or the belt, tucked between my knees.
Didn't drown. Only watched the water move.

LANDSCAPE WITH VULTURE

So this is how the ear first twitches
towards war: the vulture, pulling apart

the indiscernible animal on the neighbor's
lawn. The crowd that stills

to watch its crime, the victim
unraveled into gizzard rope.

I have seen a lot of death lately.
First the bumblebee, decapitated

in the garden, the work of some angel, a hornet,
then the squirrel with its toothpick ribs,

its chest torn open to the sky. My mother
swerved to avoid the offal stench

following my sound; I couldn't help it.
I lowed the first note, the cue

to mourn obvious and red.
And how to say I saw the bird

descending, oblivious to all
but its appetite? How to say I understood

its hunger the way all birds do:
talons out, hooked in the light.

BLOOD MOON

Night passes, brush of leg against leg, and the car
is suddenly flooded with light. Ahead of us, hanging
as if from a rusted nail, the moon, bright
as an orange. Around us, the subtleties of string
lights, dotting the December dark with red, green: electric,
fabulous. Asphalt underneath our feet, the black exterior
of want. If I listen hard enough, I think I can hear you breathe,
as if from miles away. It's as if I can't reach out and touch
you at all. The day has passed us by, the slippage of hours
spilling from my purse. Frost on the windows, my fingers
chilled from where I wiped them to see outside. Sudden heat
from the gearshift. Something in the car shifts, almost
imperceptibly. It isn't the animal desire usually makes of me, galloping
inside my chest, nor the long mournful call of the train that signals
the end of the line. Something more macabre, like the man who severed
five of his fingers in the movie we went out of our way to watch.
What was it, that which stirred him first to passion? I think I understand it
now. The desire to leave a mark on something: the sand, the lake
another character drowned in, or the sky that stood over everything,
a witness. Under the moon, the light pools in the whites of your eyes.
You look, for a moment, frightening.

AUGURY

Yes, I have seen the murmuration. The birds, dipping
themselves into night. The river so long by now we've forgotten
where it began, and if it even matters. The landscape, broken
by a startle of wings, the crows, their murder on a power line.

Yes, I have seen the sky blink its lights out. When you kissed
me that first time in the park, where we talked about your father, his
family, my mother, my family. The sun, hot and slurring on our shoulders
and we thought we were invincible in our knowledge. I learned how to say

yes, touch me, there, touch me there, your hand on my mouth, touch me
in a way that didn't sound like I was feigning desire. And for the most part,
I do not lie to you. For the most part, I render myself truthful. Isn't that
what you wanted? I'm confused. My body is an apostrophe around your body,

yes, something that indicates possession. I have never wanted someone
to love me so much, and now that I have your love, what do I do with it?

DERIVATION

Sometimes, I dream I never left that room, my underwear, my name
pushed to the side like an afterthought: a bit of mess on the plate. A man named

for God's judgment assaults me and so, a pregnancy test. A man *couldn't*
help himself, and so I called my mother, who called me everything but my name.

My mother, who named me for tradition,
for grandmothers named

after pearls, lilies, after foliage. Somewhere, the dead women
of my family rise from the grave to mother me, to call my name

into the blackening night. These women, who are so like
and unlike me it makes me cry, who share this ornamentation,

this wound that constellates out from my center,
its bad inheritance, this name

my name, which means pure. Kathryn a bird flying
into the autumn air. I watch it go, and something inside me loosens, is named.

ETYMOLOGY

"you sing it   my name"
                    —Tyree Daye

Say *Hecate*. Say *Aikaterine*. Say *Kathryn*.
Something hexing, from the Greek meaning pure,
meaning white silk slippers, meaning
the hypocritical clench of the letter K—my dead sister's
middle initial, my dead sister's middle name.
Kay. Like my brother *Karsten,* from the Greek
meaning anointed, or from the low German
meaning Christian. I do not serve God. God
does not serve me. Say *Keturah*. From the Hebrew,
meaning incense. Say she was a concubine.
Say I have lived with my hands pressed to my spine,
being opened for those who would harm me; God had
nothing to say. Say my father wanted to name me
Kassandra. Say I was unbelieved. I was
unbelieved. The mouth does not open
for that it cannot see. Say *Christine*. God hissed
in the tree of my name, his cross heavy as any father
on my shoulder digging with a heavy hand
for purchase; O Lord who has licked the salt
from my name, say *aikia.* Say my name sardonic,
my name torturous, a consecration of the clot
that killed my namesake, Margaret Kathryn;
it bubbled in her lung. My father
was riddled with them, they shone
in the glow of the scans, red and holy
they shone like jewels. Say legacy of blood.
Say upfront what you mean; I'm grown
now, can see the writing on the wall; already
the doctor and her knives have gone
to work gouging anomalies out of me; little
children. Already I am expectant.
Say *Cat*. Say *Wren*. Say bird. Say
I was anything but.

PERIOD ODE

Bloody bakery. Hothouse flower blooming red
between my thighs. Delicate handkerchief unraveling
in the wind. When I get you, I got you. Queen of pills,
of not being able to move my legs that first day, weak
in the knees like a first love and just as painful. Harbinger
of the back brace, of the coffee ice cream with brownie chunks
and cookie dough bites, of dates with myself on my couch,
watching TV, watching the numbers fluctuate on my scale
and trying not to care about the fickle nature of the body.
Horse galloping over me in a gust of heat—
Drill in the most tender parts of me—
Red stamp, currency—
That week I thought I had lost you,
and was inconsolable, you came
at the 11th hour to not make a mother
of me. His child, washed out of me
like a tide. How to thank you?

CALVARY/CAVALRY

after the painting by Marc Chagall

I, too, contain a multitude
of angles, the man's love
dulling with each thud of nail
on wood. My name means pure
in every language but mine.
A cicatrix, it taught me
to prostrate myself before men
robed in the colors of God before
my mother told me God wasn't real
and the sky sickened the green
of my love's face when I came
with all my wrath ringing
my collar gold, rinsing my face
with my father's blood. When I asked
the damnable questions, I sat ready
to string him up by his hair. I sat
ready with horses.

HORSES

I'd have known the horses anywhere, sweat-slicked
muscle and twenty hands high, all wet nose and

one crusted tooth in each of their mouths. I knew them
by their barnyard stench, their piles of shit, by their names:

Hemingway. Prince. Comet.
I never learned to ride

the way my sister rode, all legs and clear commands, riding crop
dusting the horse's flank in a steady tapping motion. In fact

one summer, I screamed because a horse stepped on
my foot and I thought I heard bone snap. For an hour, I rubbed

circles into my ankle, terrified to rotate it and be proven right.
Everyone rolled their eyes as the instructor admonished me. *Does it really*

hurt that bad? I've always been a bad animal. I've always been bad
at determining real danger, like the man who said he wouldn't hurt

me as his hand clutched a pulpy knot of my hair.
My face lit up pale in his bathroom afterwards, the blood

between my thighs red and pulsing. I checked my eyes, saw nothing
in the dark pupils except my own terror; I called it love.

I saw a horse get branded once in a movie. I could smell it, could see
the tossing of its head in fear, how it was tied down by the neck.

And then the movie where a man wakes to a horse head
in his bed and screams and screams. In both instances, I was the horse.

When I told her what happened, my mother just turned, looked at me darkly, as though through a funhouse mirror.

Congratulations, she said. *You're a woman now.*

MURDER THEORY

"Image: a meadow and then a meadow backwards."
—Bradley Trumpfheller

In the clearing, the calf can only make
a wide circle around what it does not know.
Its mother somewhere close, lowing and chewing
grass, the tags through their ears reflecting sunlight.
They have been assigned a number. They have been
given a purpose. In the clearing, a man with a knife,
advancing on the calf. It is out of the way. No one
will guess what he is doing. The man is starving,
but that doesn't mean you should have sympathy
for his situation. He is about to kill something living,
and close to its mother. For years, I cleaned my plate
of meat. I divorced what I saw from how it got there.
At a farm once, I was taught to kill a chicken. I put it
in the kill cone and watched another person cut
its throat, watched the blood come ribboning out.
The knife, sticky and feathered and sharp. People need
to eat. But—indelible is the squawk, the panicked flap
of wings. I remember saying *no*. I remember saying *stop*.
And then my mother, with her bowed head. It's not
that she didn't see. It's that she wouldn't.

FAWN

Don't look. At the head, lolling onto the highway,
at the youth of the deer bisected
at the guardrail. I counted at least ten
such animals before becoming depressed as the car lurched
upstate, past Harrisburg and its Three Mile Island.
Look at that instead. Learn something. It's okay
if you abandon things. People. Reactors.
Same old, same old. As long as
your mistakes don't take one billion to clean up, I'd wager
you're in better shape than most people. My mother laughed
the first time we sped by the site in our car; there was a movie released
shortly before shit went south at the plant: it had a line
about how an explosion there could render an area the size
of Pennsylvania permanently uninhabitable. You've got to admit
that's comedy gold, in a sort of divine timing kind of way. Or, you could think
of the fawn. I keep thinking about its mother, wondering
if she even noticed it was gone.

APPETITE

after C. K. Williams

Here was my relationship with my mother, who lived as one ought
      to have lived in her discipline: pragmatically,
a door slammed shut, an astigmatism
      on God's good eye, the one He uses or doesn't

use for watching suffering. We have both
      suffered, my mother and I. We have both cleaned our plates.
We know what it costs. I did not know her, really.
      But who ever really knows their mother?

She hated her mother, for a time. Her mother, whom I loved.
      Her mother, who called her fat and pasted pictures of obese women
on the refrigerator door to discourage her from eating. Or was that
      my grandfather? Cruelty is never singular.

Maybe that's why she said what she said. Did what she did.
      How when I was a child, I would hide candy wrappers
from her, how she gave me hell over a hidden Sprite can.
      Once, she pinched the fat between my ribs so hard

I could feel her touch for days. Even now, I forget to eat.
      I stomach the alternating current of praise, of begrudging admiration
when she can feel the sharp jut of my collarbones through
      my shirt.

But one summer, years ago, when a man I thought I loved hurt me
      in a way that seems even now unconscionable,
told me he had given me something
      told me he couldn't give me more information,

and the gynecologist had the sad, drooping eyes of a basset hound
      as he peered between my legs to assess the damage done
or not done, she held me. She peered through her thick glasses: she
      held me.

DARCY

I spend my Saturday night watching a man I liked
in middle school be bent over a table and spanked

with a riding crop in his father's play. He is an actor.
I am the audience. I have been given a ticket. I have

been assigned a seat. During the monologue,
he looks at me with the intensity of recognition.

For a moment, I blush red as an ember, grateful
for the polypropylene mask. I have not had someone look at me

like that in a long time. I thought no one would look
at me like that again: straight to the meat of me, unsparing.

I had forgotten the lush hush of a black
box theater, the cool anonymity under lights.

Being perceived unnerves me, but being ignored
is worse. Last Saturday, I saw the man

I thought I'd marry, and we passed by each other
and said nothing. He'd cut his hair. He did not look back.

It was clear he was not the man I had
loved. Desire made a door

of me. I stepped through the door. I packed my things
into a little brown suitcase, and tried not to remember

we had talked about children at one point.
How we'd make such great parents.

A friend tells me that writing about the man is akin
to scraping ink from a burning house and I'm inclined

to believe it. Not because he is beautiful to me anymore, but because
the metaphor is merely solid, and I've a penchant for taking what

was never mine to begin with. After all,
how many more original ways are there to say:

I loved you. You hurt me. And again.
You loved me. I hurt you. And again.

SELF-PORTRAIT AS TEENAGE TREE TRIMMER

after Nicky Beer

My dad would tell me stories about himself at 16,
before his kneecap was ripped off during a football game
and he settled for Michigan State and decided
Goethe was more his speed than Shakespeare was,
he'd tell me stories about being high up in the cherry
picker, and how not to hold your chainsaw. He told me
about a man he hated on the job, mean and drunk, whose name
was Chad or Martin—Wayne—something commonplace, something
I've already forgotten. How one winter, Chad or Martin—Wayne—was strolling
down a block of frozen trees to trim branches with
the chainsaw above his head until it hit a knot in the wood
and kicked back into his skull, the chainsaw above his head
until it wasn't anymore. *That poor son of a bitch,*
my dad said, shaking his still-intact head *I didn't like*
him, but no one deserves to go like that. I could think
of a few exceptions to that rule. I've become quite
the student of little violences. And sometimes, I think
of how my last name is slang for a violent profession: *pfotenhauer*
translating to paw slapper, mean teacher, lumberjack. How I once hit
someone so hard it sent their head spinning on their neck, and I felt
powerful, electric, like no one could touch me again. My hand a mouth
speaking, saying *do not touch me again.*

DAUGHTERING

after Lisa Allen Ortiz

Begin with this: the animals crowding the field.
They multiply, the deer, the bear, fox, owl, all denizens of the field.

When I was small, I chased white butterflies around our apartment block.
Not a lepidopterist so much as a child, I imagined the world was a field.

My father could only watch me, his bad leg dragging across the ground.
My father, terrified I would run into the path of a car circling the field.

My father drinks wine out of small plastic cups during happy hour.
At the facility he lives in now, there is no green, no field.

It is a matter of safety, although he doesn't see it that way: in his mind,
it is abandonment, and his cane rests by the door, and he dreams of the field

where he first learned injury: his kneecap, torn off during a football game.
He waited a week for it to heal before agreeing to surgery. A battlefield

of scar tissue now, his body, twin lines marking where the doctors cut into his shoulders,
his twice-replaced knees, the spinal cord stroke; his bones sing the field.

How many times have I compared him to a wounded animal? Made allusions
to his staccato gait and the way his hand fell heavy on my shoulder, how I fielded

the familial bond. I ventriloquized him, covered him in fur or feathers, made him into
the bear licking honey from the hive, or the fox I saw limping through the field

of our backyard that one morning, holding its broken leg to its chest with the look
of one in pain I saw so often in myself. And then, the fox startled over a fence, headed infield:

gone. These days, I am home so little; the garden is choked by weeds, blackberry
brambles, and my head and hands miles from here, in the fields

outside Laytonsville where my father taught me to drive. On trips home, I bring
my father little gifts: pots of honey and the stollen he craves at Christmas, field

his questions about who I have given my heart to now, and to what end. Every time, he looks
at me with the wonderment of a child in winter, seeing snow, snow blotting the field

and he pats my hand and calls me good. My father has never met
the person I became after the wounding: I am far enough to forget that in the field

another's body makes of me. David. Man of a thousand hides: nightjar
and black bear, snowy owl and buck. How to tell you, this far afield?

EXPLANATION ENDING WITH LARYNGEAL FRACTURE

after Bailey Cohen Vera

It wasn't that summer ended, gathered the blue skirt
of love around her waist. It wasn't that I was oiling my hair

with lemongrass, prostrating to the tincture touch
of sweetness. It wasn't the rot of the red bell

pepper, nor the first leaf to slough off the tree,
wingless. You have to understand, the sky

did not fall but the weather soured; dusk
curdled in a bowl of milk, the moon white

as the cataract on my mother's eye: a sugar bowl.
You have to understand I was tired of living

with half a tooth in my mouth,
with the constancy of hurt cutting

my tongue. It was his hand, heavy and silent
as a father on my throat, gripping; it was him.

THE SHRIKE

There is enough blood here even without
the bird. It's in the name, the genus

Lanius derived from the Latin, meaning butcher,
the name *shrike* indistinguishable from the Old English

for shriek. And how else to invite the violence
except in utterance: lunatic, incredible. The bird's call

sounding like nails down a back, something that smacks
of blood owed, the flawed nerve radiating pain, a mean rush

of feather and claw. In mating rituals, the male shrike performs this,
a dance that imitates skewering insects on thorns. They feed

each other. Before there is courtship, there must be craft, or assurance.
When he touched me, the birds overhead gathered like a hemline.

Stars pitted the sky like scars. I remember
the bruise on my arm was the size of his hand, the memory of fingers

all too visible. The physical damage was the kind that could disappear.
As if it never happened. As if you could blink and miss it.

CHIMNEY SWIFT

after Ada Limón

I thought it was a crow. Same black eye,
black thigh: a baby crow if it was anything at all.

The way its tiny talons curled around my fingers
in desperation, or maybe in pain. I had found it

by the side of the road, had taken it home after waiting
in vain for a mother to claim it. That night, I stayed up

with the bird as its chirping slowed to a peep, plied it
with water and applesauce like the internet told me to

until I could get it to the wildlife rescue in the morning.
It didn't survive, but I don't need to tell you that. And then

my mother, happening upon a stray cat that fell from a tree
on her way to work. It died too, but at this point, I'm repeating

myself. There is nothing like watching something die
slowly, and out of your control. The breath, escaping a body

in your arms. The bird's skull, so delicate in my hands. The hiss
the cat gave when my mother picked it up, enough,

and in that moment, alive. It seems we were made for this
heartbreak. Tell it to me: the bird was a crow.

HAWK COUNTRY

Miles from the place where I learned
how to walk into the soft part of a man's fist,

I am watching the night quicken over treetops.
The birds go calling home. They sweeten the nudging dark

with song while shades of blue—Prussian, Savoy, Cobalt—
brag about the forest floor. They are doing the best they can

to hasten the evening on. I'm living in it, an intruder,
small creature with clipped wings. For a moment,

I owe no allegiances. I steal an hour
for my life. No man here, no livid patch of blood burst

on my arm, no fingerprints gone yellow on the fat.
No voice in my ear telling me he'd make me cum.

And above, the hawk flies unencumbered.
He knows where he's going, and now? So do I.

Away from here, where my mother calls
from the house. I will never be from here again.

God—
had I wanted this bounty,
I would have asked for it.

IN MIDAS' COUNTRY

I was a beggar. No—that's not right.
Who can be a man on his knees in this country of gold? A swarm

of bees dispersed among the flowerbeds: one for each
dandelion in the garden, each a wealth of pollen in a black and yellow suit.

I rustled the plants, an intruder. And when I was rightly stung
by the honeybee, I was stung between the eyes, felt the skin pucker,

and covered my face. Who can compare
to richness? It was that abundance that made its mark on me. I watched

the bee in its death throes on the walk as the tiny nail of pain
radiated out from my center, consumed me. Watched the wild abandon

of the swarm and walked into it, desiring. What I desired wasn't the sweetness,
but the tendency towards sweetness, not the object of the swarm,

but its redemptive grace. And who cares who
was hurt in the process? Haven't I hurt people before, too, gone

into that hostile country where nothing grows
and tried to make a life? For myself, I take this life,

the sting and the plenty, call it by the name that whispers
in the darkest parts of me, call it lovingly, call it mine.

SEX ODE, FIVE YEARS AFTER THE ASSAULT

Listen: it was not the wine,
or the movie we didn't watch. Not the view

from his apartment balcony,
nor the projected video

on the side of the art museum
a block away, which I saw

as his arm encircled my waist
and pulled me to the velvet dark

of his bed. Not the way he held me
in that dark: so close not even light

could squeeze through the gaps between our bodies.
It wasn't his name, not his voice either, hot in my ear.

I had forgotten pleasure. I thought pleasure
had forgotten me. He kissed my knuckles

with the tenderness of a beloved
before the title beloved was given.

His voice in the dark said my name
with abandon. That was all I wanted,

the night's ear pressed to the window,
searching for sound: the cry thrown

from my throat like a bird. Watched each
of the buildings light up in the darkness:

one by one
they went.

AUBADE WITH BIRD

In the still-dark of nighttime, you
stapled a picture of the sun into the wall

before you came to bed. Boatlike, you
floated to me through the sheets. The wallpaper

edges curled up like the weekend's hungry fingers
on a hemline; I wore my party dress to sleep. Outside,

there was the beauty of the sky you belonged to:
a yellow moon dangled its hair into the streets.

The sidewalk outside was where I dropped
my childhood. There's now a bird's skeleton

beaten dull into the concrete,
the remnants of feathers splayed out like a fan.

You thought the bird was a sad thing,
but you didn't think it was me.

JONQUIL

The first night we spent together, the flowers outside
had just nudged their heads out of their stalks. It was May.
You could forgive me for thinking the world was beautiful.
Our bodies made a carnival of angles, a cathedral
of limbs, certain parts limned in gold, like ornaments. You told me,
there, in the dark, that I didn't know how to enjoy the moment,
or pleasure. Not yet anyway. My mouth at your mouth.
Your hand in my hand. Your fingers doing what fingers do
best, splayed against my hip. Your hip; my hip. In all this confusion,
we've forgotten whose is whose. Someone, (not you, never you)
told me once I was too loud, and so I became a sepulcher: quiet—
accommodating. I became a willing throat. I opened my mouth
to nothing. His cry against my silence. *Who could ask for more
in a lover,* I thought. I was younger then. I was a giver. I gave.

MANTISPIDAE

It wasn't when A found one inside her house,
  but a week later when I am sitting across from you on our first date

that I remember its name. Something in me rings like a
  bell and as you name your top three favorite bugs

I can't help but laugh. I can level with you on exactly
  this one thing. And then when you found the jumping spider

behind my toilet, forgave the fruit flies that rose in a cloud
  from my sink, I knew I liked you. Your body

something I curled around like a tongue in the dark, tasting
  the condom, taking you into the back of my throat

as between breaths, you called me a goddess, kept repeating
  your body, your body with a scientist's painful specificity. You know

your bodies. You have made behavior your study, and I consider myself
  a happy specimen. When we slept, I cradled your head

in my hands. When I sweated, you palmed a hand towards my stomach,
  followed it with your mouth. My thighs

brackets around your face. Your hand reaching deep inside me
  and coming out sticky, slicking the sheets. Your voice

in my ear, entirely other, entirely animal, the click of your jaw
  as you moved over me like a swarm—unsparing.

SICK DAY

I might not be able to smell, but you've got me googling
the Central American Giant Cave Roach, and how's that
for modern romance? In my searching, I find the female
roach can attract male roaches from long distances, and when
I text you, I wonder if you know I haven't changed my sheets.
I wonder if you knew how jellied my legs were the next day,
when I drove you to your friend's house so you could go running
with Mike. I made you toast with blackberry walnut jam. You told me
later you preferred waffles, but that's neither here nor there.
I wrote you a poem. I let you read it. And you gave me this cold,
which isn't my favorite gift in the world, but does make me think
of you, and I'm seriously considering making the 20-hour drive,
so you've got me some type of way. This could be all fever brain.
This could be something else entirely. You're the scientist; you tell me.

MUD DAUBER

In Baton Rouge, they were everywhere: a plurality
of nests dotting the underbelly of awnings, mud-
slick and gray. No wasps were to be seen in the dark, all
asleep or out finding spiders to seal in the piped
cylindrical tubes. They work alone, and they work
for their children. You told me about how their species
is a rare example of male paternal care: the females build,
the males guard the nests. We walked under them, dodging
the cockroaches that scuttled around the ground, my feet
splayed at weird angles in avoidance. You laughed at my desire
not to kill anything, to leave a place better than I found it, and it is then
I remembered how part of your job was tearing apart insects: literally,
you told me about how you ripped a termite in half to look at its gut.
Maybe there was a difference in opinion about beauty, how
to hold it, and whether or not we put it under glass. Above us,
the wasps did their mandibular, thankless work. A spider, stiffened—
paralyzed. You took my hand in your hand and pointed towards its web,
crooning into the night air: *look, look.* I could not look away. I did not.

VESPIDAE

There are no more pretenses.
My way of wanting cousins the way
a wasp clouds out from the hole
in its whitepaper nest: suddenly,
my stinger is grazing the earth's green thigh
pointed and sharp with purpose, my ocelli
breaking the day into blue fractals,
kaleidoscopes of light, and I press
a hungry mouth to the jumping spider
veins in your legs. Here is where I reach
a God convenient for us both. I have none,
do not pretend towards holy dark underthing I am
with inkdime eyes, my hard bone home clicking
under the avenues and red crawlspaces of skin. My desire
is renegade, on the lam, juiced and foaming,
the prospect of praise
buzzing my ear.

NOSTOS

Like kisses, rain on the windshield. Five minutes
into our drive, the back right tire went flat in a burst

of air. When confronted with my own inadequacy,
I have turned away from it: I couldn't help change the tire,

and so the man bent over in the tall August grass on I-10 East
and explained it to me and I stood there. When confronted

with the emerald body of the dragonfly dipping low
in the grass to find its breakfast, I chose to ignore it, all the while

wondering if dragonflies could bite you. Yes—
something had bitten me on the wrist last night, where the man's mouth

had closed over me in rapture. The day before, we awoke
to raw sewage creeping up the pipes like a thief. It was raining then,

too. Hurricane season, he told me. He took me into the garden, nodded
to the gecko on the side of the fence, and together, we watched the sky

come down in gray sheets. Once inside again, his skin flushed
as we moved tables and backpacks and piles of clothes onto whatever

counter space was available to us. We made pancakes
in his landlady's house. I crumbled butter into flour for what felt like hours.

Measured salt, tasted sugar. He touched me from behind, hands
turning in the white apron lashed about my hips. I washed dishes

and thought, *yes, this could be my life*. He drank my coffee. I wiped
the dots of dark liquid from the corner of his mouth, and we talked

about the deaths that made us capable of grief, and what
they used: the guns neither of us could ever own, the hypothetical light exiting

the apertures of our bodies. How easy to imagine a hole like that
splitting the forehead's monotony. How easy to think, *yes, that too*

could have been my life.

FRITZEL'S

When the jazz band starts up with St. James Infirmary Blues, you buy drinks for the man and his date in front of us. Brian and Denise are from Richmond, and within the span of two minutes, you forget what they do for a living, then go black out in the courtyard. I find you in a pool of your own vomit, and you apologize, won't stop apologizing. Inside: *you may search this whole wide world over, but you'll never find another sweetheart like me.* A woman from the bar who won't stop counting a thick band of bills tells me to take you somewhere that gives out banana bags and asks if you can make it that far. The smell of your sweat slicks the air. Another woman who was giving out CDs of the band insists on an ambulance. We're broke graduate students: the fact she thinks we can afford one is charming. What's the saying? *Bless your heart.* As I push you into the Uber, a woman wearing a snake around her hips flies by on a skateboard. The glass of the sex shop where we picked out a paddle together blazes a hot, stunning pink. You rock against the glass of the car window. You cover your eyes. Some things I guess you can't believe unless you see them.

ON DEFEAT

On the highway outside Metairie, we passed graveyards
jutting out of the ground like hip bones. You told me
something about floods and corpses; how the cities
of the dead would swell at sea level if given the chance.
How the solution was above ground tombs, and about how
one of your professors specialized in the elaborate work
of corpse recovery in disasters, making sure no bodies moved
around unsupervised. At the bar that night, I almost ordered
a corpse reviver. To be funny. To be cute. And I would've too,
if I thought you could appreciate it. But you were three sheets
to the wind and I kneeled in your vomit in the bar's courtyard
to help you to your feet and still you did not love me.

INVENTORY

Around the table at Chili's, we talk casually
about our childhood cruelties. How a boy
in fourth grade crushed the snail
our group of girls had formed around
with cupped hands, desperate to protect.
We squealed, marveled at the broken shell
in shock, the splay of its slug body on the concrete.
I'd never seen death before. You could forgive me
for thinking it was a clean thing. And the boy
walked off in the direction of the music building
untouched, where the notes of a distant cello sounded
and our choir teacher stood, taping his foot. I looked
the boy up the other day: he's getting a law degree, and his face
looks the same as it did in fourth grade: pinched thing,
the first I'd ever hit with my fist. And then E
tells us about the lizards she used
to catch and feed to the whir of an HVAC,
listen to the soft thunks of their bodies
becoming chunks spit onto the carpet.
I didn't ask how many she killed this way,
but I don't think she could count them.
I couldn't count the spiders I've washed
down the bathtub drain in fear, the ants my brother
burned under a 7-Eleven Slurpee cup with the hot
July sun and a magnifying glass, the smoking
corpses on the neighbor's drive. I've kicked
over anthills, plugged a wasp's nest with lemon
extract and watched it fall, drowned fruit flies
in apple cider vinegar and dish soap, and at this point
who can tell the difference between confession
and resurrection? There are too many things I've hurt
because I was frightened, and too many things
I can't account for.

STURGEON MOON

Technically, this is cheating: this moon still days away from flooding the earth with light. This moon still sleeping while we slept, curled around each other like an ear. I do not possess you: you've made that abundantly clear. Days later, on a night where I cannot sleep, you call me, and the first words out of the machine are *can you see it from your bed?* I pretend I can, my face turned away from the window, my eyes closed. I pretend I can see it, and so I feel close to you. I imagine the flowers in your garden unfurling under the night's silvery gaze, the roaches and earthworms in your compost bin squirming happily under the piles of rotting fruit, the remnants of the cherry pie I made you broken down into manageable pieces. In the kitchen where I rolled out the dough, wiped my hands crusted with flour on my bare thighs, you watched me. Sugar in my hair. Outside, it rained. You couldn't see the moon.

THE KISSING TREES

Hard to unsee it: two tree trunks joined in midair.
You tell me this is why the crepe myrtle is called

a kissing tree, and that's easier on the tongue than
calling it inosculation, which means the same thing

but sounds harsher somehow: a punishment, clinical. All evening,
I have lived with the inconstancy of your attention: here

your hand in my hand, a minute later, that same hand lost to me
as you peer into the dark crevices between buildings, searching

for I don't know what, but you name the trees as we walk past them:
crepe myrtle, live oak gone shaggy with Spanish moss. An acolyte,

you came to this place with a fascination that lies beyond me. The day
before I leave, and Baton Rouge begins to fade into a hot

August memory, we stop by the side of the road so you
can gather the wood of those same trees we walked under.

Your utility knife unfolds into an instrument of many purposes,
the tiny saw blade so hot by the time you finish cutting, it hurts

to touch. At home, you sit in your chair, begin to skin the bark back
with long, methodical strokes. It isn't hard to imagine what else you can do

with your hands; I know what you can do. In bed, your mouth hangs
over me like a moon, your fingers disappeared into the space

between our bodies. Is it here where I say you kissed me there? I hunger
for your body the way I hunger for most things: desperately, a palm

to your chest, to your cheek. I am miles
from you now. The missing is no less potent.

DANAINAE

Early autumn around my shoulders like a shawl,
and in New York, the leaves begin their slow turn

towards death, begin blushing how I blushed
as your mouth slid towards the soft juncture

of my neck and shoulder. Everyone looks better
in the dark, in minimal lighting, in summer swelter.

We were no exception. No less beautiful for having been
brief with each other's bodies, but we looked better

in the dark pocket of the moment. In the early dawn
your hand crept up my back to light on my shoulder

like I was something delicate, or precious. Your red beard
between my hands, and then in other places. Outside,

the clouds were brushed across the sky like a white
cat's fur standing on end; a ghost

in motion. And when I flew down to you, I had the hope
of someone enamored, a little crazy with lust. We spent days

wrapped in the cocoon of each other's body. The thing
between us was newly formed and fragile, capable of breaking

open and revealing something missing: a wing, an
antenna. A figment: something already dead. How miserable

to be proven right. And as I leave the library, a single monarch
flutters over the pebbled stone. And I won't tell you about it.

AUBADE

with a line from Frannie Lindsay

You too might, in the holiest hour
of your life, reach for me. Who's to say

when that will be? It could be your deathbed,
with your family gathered around you, a wife

with stringy brown hair and a dog that chews
your slippers. Or it could be tomorrow,

while you fuck your latest woman, kiss her
leg as you hoist it over your shoulder. There

are angles to consider: anything looks holy
if you put the right hat on it, give it the right

garb. Or maybe, the holiest hour was in that first
night, already past wishing. I was no animal, but

someone simply naked in bed with you, face slackened
with sleep, vein of drool connecting cheek to pillow.

The day had not broken open like an egg
or an unkept promise. Dawn made its lazy overtures,

but stood outside the door. In the dark
and hushed room where once you touched

me, you pulled on your clothes, and did not look back
to see if I was awake. This is not a story about love. It is, however,

about someone you left behind. And I make a good saint,
or at least something holy: I make no complaints.

I make no sound at all.

CONSIDERATIONS

after Mahmoud Darwish

Consider the yellow jackets gathering in a swarm
around your AC unit. Consider the fruit flies nesting
in the haven of your garbage can. The maggots

crawling over your rubber gloves as you destroyed
what they built trying to live. The ants, marching
rank and file towards your recycling bin, taking bits

of crumbs back for their famished queen.
Consider the killing, then consider gentleness: when
the wasp is trapped in your window,

maybe put it in a cup and return it to the world. Do not
let it die the slow death. Consider death,
the portal to that country where everyone

has your mother's face. Consider your mother, how she bore
you. Consider that you almost left this world
and yet, you came back. Consider the bloom

of insomnia in your father's eye: a cataract, a clot.
Your matching bloodshot. Consider again your father,
how he has lost everything

but you.

ACKNOWLEDGMENTS

A million thank yous to the editors of these publications, in which the following poems first appeared, sometimes in different iterations:

Bellevue Literary Review: "Driving to Meadville"
Blue Earth Review: "Inventory"
Crazyhorse: "The Hyrtl Skull Collection"
Ethel: "Derivation," "Calvary/Cavalry"
Jabberwock Review: "In the Morgue"
Memorious: "Landscape with Vulture"
Meridian: "Etymology"
Milkweed Literary Magazine: "Aubade with Bird"
Moon City Review: "Darcy"
Moot Point Magazine: "Aubade"
Ponder Review: "The Kissing Trees"
Raleigh Review: "Prayer [Approaching twenty-five…]," "Pastoral with Birds"
Stone Canoe: "Self-Portrait as Moirologist"
Superstition Review: "Prayer [Like this, the dead elk,]," "Murder Theory"
The Lovers Literary Journal: "Explanation Ending with Laryngeal Fracture"
The Lindenwood Review: "The Art Park"
The Missouri Review: "Horses," "Hawk Country," "Augury," "Jonquil"
Up the Staircase Quarterly: "Nostos"

A selection of these poems appeared in the chapbook *Small Geometries,* published by Ethel Zine & Micro Press in April/May 2023.

An earlier version of the poem "Vespidae" won the 2020 Bain-Swiggett Poetry Prize.

"Inventory" placed as a poetry runner-up in the 2022 Dog Daze Poetry Contest from *Blue Earth Review.*

"In Midas' Country" borrows its title from Sylvia Plath's "In Midas' Country."

THANKS

It takes a village to raise a book, and mine is not so much a village so much it is an entire metropolis. Firstly, an eternity of gratitude to Courtney LeBlanc and Riot in Your Throat for selecting this manuscript out of the submission queue and giving it a life.

This book would not exist had it not been for Sara Potocsny. Sara: thank you for your friendship and your love. Similarly, this book would not exist without the generosity of the Syracuse University MFA program in creative writing. I would like to thank the tremendous poetry faculty for their expertise and support: Brooks Haxton, Mary Karr, Chris Kennedy, and Bruce Smith, the best stewards my work could ask for. To my incredible cohort, Mary DiPrete, Anthony Vicente Ornelaz, Jasmine Tabor, and Laura Traverse: thank you for your brilliance, your commitment to craft and community. It's been one of the great privileges of my life to be your peer.

I couldn't ask for better friends: Emily Aquino, Catie Beveridge, Natalia Belchikov, Hayley Bowen, Caleb Brown, Rachel Bruce, J. Bryant, Gwynne Dulaney, Susannah Duncan, Marit Eiler, Natalie El-Eid, Jonah Evans, Ros Fettig, Julia Frederick, Aiyana Glauser, Karina Gonzalez, Isabel Hildesheim, Brian Holmes, Jezebel Jackson, Larry Kaplun, Divya Kirti, Delia Landers, Ariel Levchenko, Reuben Gelley Newman, Ocean Noah, Gaynor Norcott, Libby Otto, Joe Phipps, Olivia Russo, Kaden St. Onge, Kimberly Stuart, Alexis Tang, Kate Weiler, Haolun Xu, Jill Zimmerman. A huge thank you to the poetry-prose-posse: Taylor Garrison, Samantha Pearl Tropper, Veronica Walton, Katelyn Winter.

I would not be a poet without Veena Roberson, my high school English teacher. Ms. Roberson, thank you for being the best, and for all your support over the years.

To my mentors, my lighthouses, the safe harbors I return to: Julia Kolchinsky Dasbach, Thomas Devaney, Mary Karr (again), Airea D. Matthews, Bruce Smith (again and again). You teach me how to be a better human and a better artist every day; my life has been incredibly blessed to have you in it.

To my therapist, Dr. Kaufman, thank you for our work together over the years. You've seen me at my worst, and for not shying away from it, I am grateful to you.

To my parents, my grandparents: I am so lucky to be yours. I write to make you proud. To my large, incredible family: you are in everything I do.

To those who inspired these poems: you know who you are.

Finally, to Mikaela Cajigal, who remains the reason for everything and anything: the best muse and the greatest friend.

ABOUT THE AUTHOR

Kathryn Bratt-Pfotenhauer is the author of poetry collection *Bad Animal* and the chapbook *Small Geometries*. The recipient of a Pushcart Prize and awards from Bryn Mawr College and the Ledbury Poetry Festival, their poetry and fiction has been published or is forthcoming in *Giving Room Mag*, the *Missouri Review*, the *Adroit Journal*, *Crazyhorse*, *Poet Lore*, *Beloit Poetry Journal*, and others. They have received support from the Seventh Wave and Tin House. They attend Syracuse University's MFA program.

ABOUT THE PRESS

Riot in Your Throat is an independent press
that publishes fierce, feminist poetry.

Support independent authors, artists, and presses.

Visit us online:
www.riotinyourthroat.com

Printed in the USA
CPSIA information can be obtained
at www.ICGtesting.com
JSHW042126010823
45657JS00001B/1

9 781736 138687